UTOPIANISM IN POLITICS

AJAY VAID

ISBN 979-888555163-2

Contents

Preface

Utopia, or the concept of the perfect society, is an essential component of political philosophy. It is focused on the critique and improvement of existing society. This is the central theme of Thomas More's Utopia. Both negatively and favorably, the concept of utopia has become popular in social and political philosophy. Some theorists perceive a path from paradise to dictatorship, with violence as an unavoidable component. Others view it as inextricably linked to freedom and essential in the battle against totalitarianism. Several scholars have suggested that utopianism has ended after the fall of communism in Eastern Europe and the former Soviet Union. It hasn't; utopias are still being written and intentional communities are being established in the hope of a better existence.

CHAPTER ONE

INTRODUCTION

INTRODUCTION

In the section Utopianism in Politics we shall deal with the utopian aspects of the political ideas and philosophy of great political thinkers beginning from Plato to the present day. The interesting aspect of their thought system is, except Thomas More (1478-1535) whose work Utopia was published in 1515, none has directly or categorically used the word utopia or referred to it. Notwithstanding the political philosophers or ideas of many of them can reasonably be classified as utopian in nature. These political thinkers have built up their political, social and economic analysis in the context of practical situations. But the structure of their analysis and the conclusions they drew were, from the standpoint of reality, impractical. The recommendations they made could never be translated into reality and that is why we call their suggestions and recommendations utopian. The logic and arguments they made are in many cases undeniable. But the mere fact is that political reality does not always stand on arguments or logic. Plato was so much perturbed by the events of his time that he practically lost all faith on the state structure that existed around him and this led him to suggest an alternative state structure or political system which is popularly known as ideal state. But the elements of ideal state are absolutely unattainable. For example, there can never occur communism in wives and children, Even communism in property is simply an impossibility. Plato is reasonably regarded by many as the father of utopianism because he laid the foundation stone of utopianism in his concept of ideal state.

CHAPTER TWO

ORIGIN AND DEFINITION

ORIGIN AND DEFINITION

The origin of the term utopia can be traced to More's book Utopia who prepared the book on the basis of the Greek eu topos which means good place. Some thinkers believe that there is another origin of the word utopia and in this case it is also Greek. It is ou topos and this means no place. Hence the difference in Greek is ou and eu. It has been assumed by the philosophers/thinkers that a utopia or a definite place exists nowhere. It is simply an imaginary place. At least Thomas More thought so. The advocates of utopian thought believe that an ideal place or political organisation can be set up in real world and when they make plans and programme, that approach is called utopianism. Let us define it in the words of Heywood (Political Theory, p. 366). "Utopianism is a style of social theorising that develops a critique of the existing order by constructing a model of an ideal or perfect alternative".

Utopianism, therefore, can be considered as a criticism of the existing system of society or state and a recommendation of a perfect future social/political system. The author of the article in Oxford Concise Dictionary of

Politics defines it: "A disposition to embrace the vision of an alternative society from which present social evils have been eradicated and in which there is complete human fulfilment and well-being through the attainment of perfect justice, freedom equality and/or other ideals formulated by the utopian authors". Utopianism, therefore, stands for something which is perfect or ideal.

CHAPTER THREE

RISE AND DECLINE OF UTOPIANISM

Rise and Decline of Utopianism

Utopianism registered its appearance in the writings of Plato and Aristotle and its flowering continued up to the end of nineteenth century when Marx's scientific socialism, concept of classless society, and withering of state drew the attention of the scholars of both the hemispheres. In the first few decades of the twentieth century utopianism was faced with decline. Especially Marxism was challenged by several, trends of political thought; the most important of them was behaviouralism. Marxism was challenged not for its context of utopianism but its approach to capitalism. In the 1960s and 1970s, another utopianism surfaced in the political and academic worlds and it was feminism or Femi the nist movement. The feminist movement challenged the male domination in academic and political fields and even some feminists called it male chauvinism. There occurred also a slight revival of utopianism in the thought and propaganda of neoliberalism which made its appearance in the latter half of the twentieth century. Finally, we find that utopianism came to be neglected and simultaneously anti-utopianism or non-utopianism was encouraged. Students, political scientists, and academics were disillusioned with utopianism with utopian thought. It was believed by them that utopianism had completely failed to provide any solution to the burning questions that were tormenting the minds of people and, it could not be an alternative to existing doctrines and models. All these adequately signaled the decline of utopianism.

CHAPTER FOUR

CHARACTERISTICS OF UTOPIANISM

Characteristics of Utopianism

There are several features of utopianism or utopian political thought:

1. Utopian thought is a critique of the existing political system, structure and functioning of the state or political organisation.

2. It suggests alternative scheme or programme which is designed to replace the present system by a new system or structure.

3. Utopianism aims at abolishing inequality, injustice, oppression, exploitation, want, conflict, violence etc. It thinks of avoiding violence. Utopia is a place of the mortal world with the basic features of heaven.

4. It vehemently opposes the existing system because of its embodiment of all types of imperfection. In place of such a system utopianism thinks of a perfect social system.

5. Utopianism believes that the present social and political structure does not create ample scope for the comprehensive development of human personality and the good and finer qualities which an individual possesses. But it is essential that the best qualities of individuals shall get

the opportunity to thrive and for that reason the system that fails to do the job must be replaced by another.

6. In the present social and political system there is a clear distinction between public and private and very often this creates an atmosphere of conflict which is absolutely unhealthy. Also jeopardises the progress of society.

7. Heywood has drawn our attention to another feature of utopian political thought. He says: It goes "beyond conventional political thought and addressed wider psycho-social and even psycho-sexual issues" (p. 365).

8. Utopianism is to some extent emotionally surcharged. It is based more on emotion than on logic and reason. The present structure pains the heart of utopian thinkers and they planned for a future perfect human society.

CHAPTER FIVE

UTOPIANISM IN GREEK POLITICAL THOUGHT

Utopianism in Greek Political Thought

Though utopianism can be traced in the writings of several thinkers of twentieth century its earliest exposition can be found in the writings of Plato (B. C. 427-347) and partially in the work of his famous disciple Aristotle (BC 384-322). Plato's The Republic is the best example of utopianism. He, being completely disgusted with existing political system of contemporary Greek city-states, planned for an ideal state whose aim was to free the citizens and administration from the evils. The entire structure of his ideal state was full of utopian thoughts and schemes. Plato's philosopher-king, communism in wives and children and even his education system are nothing but symbols of utopianism. Plato also thought of communism of property. During the last more than two thousand years nowhere in the world Plato's political schemes have been implemented. As an ideal Plato's scheme of ideal state is very attractive no doubt but since its implementation has not invoked our enthusiasm we call it utopian. Aristotle also thought of an ideal state. But his ideal state is also shrouded with unreal or utopian thoughts and schemes. He conceived that only a polity could be ranked with ideal state and in such a state there cauld not reside any form of inequality and injustice. By inequality he meant inequality in wealth, property, opportunity and status. Polity would consist of the people belonging to middle class. But such a conception of polity is completely impractical. It is because all the people of the polity cannot have same or almost same amount of property which neither too much or too less.

CHAPTER SIX

UTOPIANISM IN MIDDLE AGES

Utopianism in Middle Ages

In the Middle Ages several thinkers dreamt of setting up or organising a political community whose purposes were both political and moral or ethical and this double approach laid the foundation of utopianism in politics. The most important personality in this period was Saint Augustine (354-430). St. Augustine imagined that there were two cities-one was situated in heaven and the other in this mortal world that is earth. Only gods were the inhabitants of the city of heaven and the mortal beings, that is human beings, live in the city situated in the earth. According to Augustine the City of God is the ideal place where there is no scope of sin, selfish behaviour etc. The heart and mind of the heavenly city is so pure that their character is not tainted like the character of the people living in the mortal world. Hence he concluded that place like city of God is to be created. Augustine's city of God is comparable with Plato's ideal state. The City of God, in all good, moral, and ethical senses, is absolutely ideal. The rulers of earthly cities must try to set up states or cities like the city of God. Following Aristotle, Marsillius of

Padua (1280-1349) wanted to set up an ideal state whose foundation would be morality, ethics and religion. Christianity would control and guide almost all the aspects and activities of state. In his idea spirituality, religion, morality and idealism were mixed with politics. In other words, all these would constitute the foundation of state and politics. The other thinkers expressed more or less same view. To sum up, the politics of Middle Ages was completely enveloped by, utopianism.

CHAPTER SEVEN

ROUSSEAU AND UTOPIANISM

Rousseau and Utopianism

Rousseau's political ideas offer us a clear example of political utopianism. He thought of setting up a political organisation whose main purpose would be to revive morality, ethics and idealism which prevailed in the state of nature and this could be done through the social contract. He said : "The problem is to find a form of association which will defend and protect with the whole common force the persons and goods of each associate, and in which each, while uniting himself with all, may still obey himself alone and remain as free as before" (G. D. H. Cole edited Social Contract. p. 12). Rousseau calls the state a moral person whose chief function is to make all citizens moral and ideal. Rousseau believed that in the state of nature men were moral, ideal and ethical. The progress of civilisation destroyed all these qualities. So for the revival of these, a new and moral civil society was badly needed. To make a state moral, ideal and ethical is not sheer utopian. Rousseau also proposed for creating a popular sovereignty and in his account it would act through the general will. All the adult citizens would meet periodically in an open space for deliberations and the will which would come out of it would be the basis of general will that is sovereignty. He has also said that general will aims at general or common good and in it there is no place of a particular will. Only utopianism can think such ideas. Rousseau believed that his men would rise above all sorts of parochial interests. We conclude that in nowhere of the world and in no age such thing will occur.

CHAPTER EIGHT

UTOPIAN SOCIALISTS

Utopian Socialists

The utopian impulse and ideas found their ways in the writings of the utopian socialists—Robert Owen (1771-1858), Fourier (1772-1837) and St. Simon (1760-1825). All of them were precursors of Marxian socialism. These socialist thinkers are called utopian because of the fact that the methods suggested by them for setting up of a socialist society were out and out impractical. Engels for that reason called

them utopian. All the three socialist thinkers in the core of their heart believed that by changing the mind, heart and attitude of the capitalists a new socialist society could be created. The change in heart and behaviour would lead the capitalists to work whole-heartedly for the general welfare and upliftment of the poor people and workers. They will refrain themselves from exploitation. Robert Owen spent his life-long saving and property to set up a society which would be free from all sorts of exploitation, misery, oppression. But he could not succeed. He appealed to his fellow-industrialists and friends to free the workers from exploitation and oppression. Charles Fourier made numerous attempts to create an ideal and perfect society. Saint Simon was convinced that capitalists' lust for excessive profit and urge to accumulate more and more wealth were the prime causes of unbound misery of the working class. Saint Simon believed that the change of heart and activities of the capitalists could bring about a change in the distress of the workers. In this way all the three utopian socialists landed themselves on impractical programmes of a new society.

CHAPTER NINE

UTOPIANISM OF MARX

Utopianism of Marx

In the long list of utopian political thinkers Karl Marx tops the list though this may be contested by his followers. Marx's analysis of the evolution of human society, the analysis of its nature, the class struggle, exploitation of workers, growing miseries of the working class, repetition of crises of capitalism etc. are all based on scientific analysis and based on historical facts. But his prediction about the fate of capitalism-that is, its imminent collapse, capture of state by the proletarians, establishment of classless society and, finally, the withering away of bourgeois state are treated as utopian. In nowhere of the world has Marxian socialism been established and state has withered away. Though it is claimed that in the erstwhile Soviet Union socialism was established, there is a large amount of doubt about its exact nature. Even it was not Marxian or scientific socialism. Plato imagined of an ideal state which was supposed to cater all the needs especially the moral requirements of its citizens, Rousseau's state which was a moral person was meant to be a moral person and to provide liberty and Marx's classless society had the objective to free the toiling masses and teeming millions from the various oppressions. There is a close link in all these declarations—they are all utopians. Marx offered us an inexorable logic-it is common people will revolt against the oppression which will precipitate the collapse of bourgeois state. Beginning from the middle of the nineteenth century up to the end of twentieth century people have agitated but the state structure has remained intact.

CHAPTER TEN

UTOPIANISM IN LIBERALISM

Utopianism in Liberalism

Liberalism is also not free from utopian thought and content. If we go through the tendency and objective of liberalism, it will be quite clear that it has a biasness for utopianism. Liberalism, we know, has declared its commitment to individualism and supreme importance of the freedom of individuals. It further believes that individuals are capable of doing their own good and welfare through their own efforts. In this context liberalism forcefully asserts that in both political and economic affairs the individuals shall be left alone and the state intervention shall be reduced to the minimum. In different ages liberalism has assumed new colours but the supremacy of the individuals has remained almost intact. Today we, after considering all the aspects of social development, come to the conclusion that even the modified approach of liberalism is utopian. Liberalism advocates laissez-fair and free market economy. Laissez-faire, today, is to some extent an absolute concept because during the last more than one century it has proved its inefficiency. No country can implement all the principles of laissez-faire and it is not possible. In many cases the state is forced to intervene in the economic process. Hence development through laissez-faire is nothing but a day-dream concept. Market economy is stridently advocated and it has been asserted it is the only way to develop society. But unrestricted market economy or free market is not a master key with which all the locks can be unlocked. The intervention of state becomes inevitable. On experience it has been found that undiluted liberalism is no solution to problems with which we are faced.

CHAPTER ELEVEN

THEORY OF UTOPIANISM

Theory of Utopianism

If we go through the writings of the utopian thinkers we shall find that there are certain assumptions in their writings. They conceived of restructuring of the existing society and for this reason Heywood (Political Theory p. 368) has said that political utopianism is defined more by its structure than its content.

Almost all the utopians assumed :

1. The society must be free from injustice, coercion, inequality, morality and ethics.This is specially evident in Plato's Republic and Aristotle's Politics. Plato thoughtthat the political systems of his contemporary Greek city-states were not only corrupt but violated, in the name of democracy, the basic norms of liberty, rights, equality and justice. In these city-states there was no place of idealism, ethics and moral values. These must be restored at any cost and the revival is possible only in an ideal state. Aristotle's polity also aimed at the same objective.

2. Most of the utopians conceived of building up state structure which would be free from poverty, exploitation, oppression etc. and for this it is necessary to build up a

perfect society. But for such a society there shall be abundance of all types of consumption goods which means the abolition of poverty and eradication of injustice. Not only all the goods used for consumption shall be abundantly available, there shall be material progress. In other words, the society shall be materially well-developed. Marx and Engels thought that only in socialism there can be a guarantee of the abundance of material and consumption goods and when that happens, the society can rightly be called perfect. The material progress is possible if all the sources of production and methods of distribution are handed over to the responsibility of the state which means the nationalization of the economy. It is a utopian concept because the Bolshevik party in Russia took this step but could not set up a perfect society ensuring the abundance of both material and consumption goods. Even people had no full access to rights, liberty, and equality. This drawback, it is alleged, was the main factor of the collapse of Soviet regime in 1991.

3. Utopianism highlights the harmony among all sections of the people in society. It has been assumed by the utopian socialists if poverty is abolished and the abundance of material and consumption goods is fully assumed, the brotherhood or harmony among all sections of society would not remain a faraway concept. It has been argued by political utopianism that the main cause of conflict or disharmony among the people is poverty or the juxtaposition of poverty and opulence. If this is removed or considerably reduced the source of conflict would be nipped in the bud. The system of private property is the main source of conflict and all sorts of imperfection. But since its abolition is not an easy task, force is inevitable. The state authority by applying coercive measures shall

force the property owners to surrender a part of the excess property to the state which will be distributed among the propertyless men. There is utopianism in the entire concept. Private property is a reason for conflict but not the only reason and the nationalisation of resources cannot ensure justice and perfection. We get this lesson from past experiences of the former Soviet Union. Though private property is a cause of imperfection its removal does not lie in the abolition of the property system. The socialists were under the influence of the wrong conception which is called utopian.

4. The liberals think that competition among men, groups and institutions canfinally lead to the creation of a perfect society. On the other hand, it is the belief of the socialists that competition is the primary reason of conflict and this leads to disharmony and loss of brotherhood. These are definitely not the criteria of a perfect society. Both liberalism and socialism are utopian in their approach to competitionand perfection. Competition can never be a precursor to perfection though in a perfect society there can be competition. But this competition does not mean to gain ascendency in management of social and political affairs but competition in academic and intellectual affairs. This type of competition is never a barrier to perfection. We hold the view that too much emphasis on competition and its imaginary.role in making a perfect society is utopian. On the contrary, socialist's idea that competition is cause of conflict and its abolition can bring about a perfection are also not correct. Conflict is a subject of psychology and is related is human nature. Its cause and role are very often oversimplified. Moreover, the idea of a perfect society is to some extent utopian. What do we mean by perfection? It is an ethical, moral, or ideal concept and

it varies from person to person and society to society. We cannot reach a definite conclusion about it.

5. Utopianism promises complete emancipation and unlimited freedom. In both feudal and capitalist societies the serfs and industrial workers were exploited by the landlords and capitalists, respectively. They were also oppressed. Marx and Engels wanted a complete abolition of this human practice perpetrated by a microscopic section of society and in order to do this abolition of feudalism and capitalism was suggested. However, as a part of social evolution, the feudal system was abolished by social forces such as advent of capitalism, irrelevance of feudalism in new economic system. Marxism promises that only socialism or its higher form communism (Marx thought so) could promise a complete emancipation of all exploited people. After emancipation all will get the opportunity to enjoy unlimited freedom. In no society is there complete emancipation. Exploitation in any form can there be in any society and its abolition is simply a utopian idea. A man may be free from economic exploitation but as Prof. Ernest Barker said he may be victim of superstition or religious diktat. Where this exists, one cannot say of any emancipation. Similarly, "unbounded freedom" is not possible. For the better and wider freedom, certain laws, and restrictions are essential. Thus socialists' claim of unbounded freedom and complete emancipation are not real concepts, they are absolutely utopian ideas. At least practical experience tells us so. State intervention is an important precondition of freedom.

CRITICISM OF UTOPIANISM

Criticism by the Conservatives

The conservative thinkers have criticized utopianism in politics on several grounds and some of these are :

1. One of the foundations of utopianism is human nature is perfect. But the conservatives argue that human nature is "imperfect and perfectible" (Heywood, p. 372). According to conservatism the human beings are selfish and are guided by irrational ideas and thoughts. In such a situation utopianism cannot be successful. Human societies are formed with individuals whose motives and characters are questionable. With the help of such individuals, a perfect and utopian society cannot be constituted. Marx's classless society/state is out and out a utopian concept. The critics are of opinion that even if it were possible to form such a state that can never last long because imperfect human nature will precipitate its fall.

2. The conservatives further object that models for a future society can easily be prepared, but the problem is the justifiability of the model. That is, how far such a model is justifiable or how far it is applicable—that must be properly judged. It is unfortunate that the great utopian thinkers did

not pay proper attention to this aspect. They were so much enamored by idealist thought that they practically did not consider the real situation. This is perfectly applicable to all utopian philosophers from Plato to Marx. Even the feminists and a large number of liberals were victims of impractical concepts.

Other Criticisms

Two political scientists—Karl Popper and Isaiah Berlin have criticized the utopian concept of politics. Explaining Popper's standpoint Heywood (Political Theory, p. 372) maintains that "for Popper, utopianism was dangerous and pernicious because it is self-defeating and leads to violence". The utopians select the ultimate aim of state or society and in the light of this they suggest/recommend means or methods to reach that end. It has been alleged that the utopias have not analyzed the rationality of the means and even the goals. For example, Plato imagined an ideal state and simultaneously prepared its blueprint. But such an ideal state could never be achieved. He was also to some extent suspicious of the attainment of an ideal state. Marx and Engels perhaps did not know that the setting up of a classless society was simply an impossibility. Despite this, they and some of their followers forcefully argued for it. Utopianism misleads the people. It never provides a correct guideline for the general mass. It poses a rosy picture. This is not the correct way. Popper also observed that utopianism may invite violence. The end of state or political science and as well as the blueprint is not based on rationality. Naturally on these two issues conflicts among the people may crop up. Popper has said that the emergence of conflict is natural and this conflict may be a potential source of violence. Both the ends and means may be interpreted differently.

Isaiah Berlin has criticized utopianism from another angle. He says that monism or monistic tendencies are involved in utopianism and, according to Berlin, it is derived from Enlightenment. Enlightenment advocates for universal reason and from this tendency utopianism have argued for monism or universalism. This is particularly evident in Plato's ideal state, Rousseau's concepts of a moral person and general will, and Marx's idea of a classless society. These concepts practically make no room for alternative schemes or arguments. Marx believed that a classless society was inevitable. Plato thought that the ideal state was the only solution to the numerous evils from which his contemporary Greek city-states were suffering. In Rousseau's account general will is infallible and symbolizes the welfare of all people. Hence all people must show their unconditional obligation to the general will. These arguments are not acceptable. The foundation of any society must be in all senses pluralist. All shades of opinion must have the opportunity to ventilate their viewpoints. But for in utopian politics, this finds no place. "Berlin asserted that conflicts of values are intrinsic to human life, not only will people always disagree about the ultimate ends of life, but each human being struggles to find a balance between incommensurable values. Such a view demonstrates that utopia is in principle, impossible" (Heywood, op. cit., p. 373).

Bibliography

- EmileDurkheim, Le Socialisme; sa définition, ses débuts; la doctrine saint-simonienne, Paris, F. Alcan, 1928.
- Frank and Fritzie Manuel, Utopian Thought in the Western World, Cambridge, Mass., Harvard University Press, 1979.
- Robert A. Nisbet, The Sociological Tradition, New York, Basic Books, 1966.
- Women in utopia. The Ideology of gender in the American Owenite communities, Bloomington, Indianapolis, Indiana University Press, 1990.
- Carl J Guarneri, The Utopian alternative. Fourierism in nineteenth-century America, Ithaca, and London, Cornell University Press, 1991.
- http://onlinebooks.library.upenn.edu/webbin/book/lookupname?key=Cole%2C%20G%2E%20D%2E%20H%2E%20%28George%20 Douglas%20Howard%29%2C%201889%2D1959
- http://mgdc-chararisharief.com/elearn/Political%20Theory-1stSem.pdf
- http://www.mim.ac.mw/books/Andrew%20Heywood%20-%20Politics%202nd%20edition.pdf